A Visit to
BRAZIL

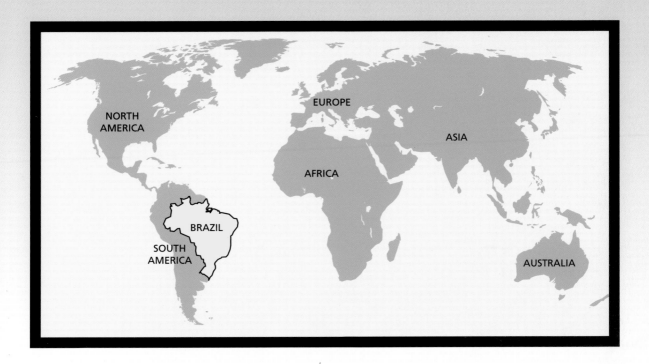

Peter & Connie Roop

Heinemann Interactive Library
Des Plaines, Illinois

© 1998 Reed Educational & Professional Publishing
Published by Heinemann Interactive Library,
an imprint of Reed Educational & Professional Publishing,
1350 East Touhy Avenue, Suite 240 West
Des Plaines, IL 60018

Printed in Hong Kong by Wing King Tong Co., Ltd.
Designed by AMR
Illustrations by Art Construction

02 01 00 99 98
10 9 8 7 6 5 4 3 2 1

Library of Congress Cataloging-in-Publication Data

Roop, Peter.
    Brazil / by Peter and Connie Roop.
        p.   cm. -- (A visit to)
    Includes bibliographical references and index.
    Summary: Describes many aspects of the largest country in South
America, including its land, landmarks, homes, food, clothes,
schools, sports, celebrations, and arts.
    ISBN 1-57572-125-2 (lib. bdg.)
    1. Brazil--Description and travel--Juvenile literature.
[1. Brazil.] I. Roop, Connie. II. Title. III. Series: Roop,
Peter, Visit to.
F2517.R66   1998
981--DC21   97-37236
                                                      CIP
                                                       AC

Acknowledgements
The Publishers would like to thank the following for permission to reproduce photographs:
LUPE CUNHA: pp. 20, 26; Hutchison Library: p. 23, Errington p. 12, J. Horner p. 9, C. Macarthy p. 22,
J. von Puttkamer p. 5; Tony Morrison: pp. 10, 11, 13, 16, 17, 25, 27, South American Pictures pp. 6,
14, 19, 28, 29; Trip: S. Grant pp. 7, 24, T. Lester p. 18, C. Phillips p. 15, J. Wender p. 21; ZEFA: J. Ramid p. 8

Cover photograph reproduced with permission of Sue Cunningham Photographic.

Our thanks to Rob Alcraft for his comments in the preparation of this book.

Every effort has been made to contact holders of any material reproduced in this book.
Any omissions will be rectified in subsequent printings if notice is given to the Publisher.

Any words appearing in bold, **like this**, are explained in the Glossary.

Contents

Brazil

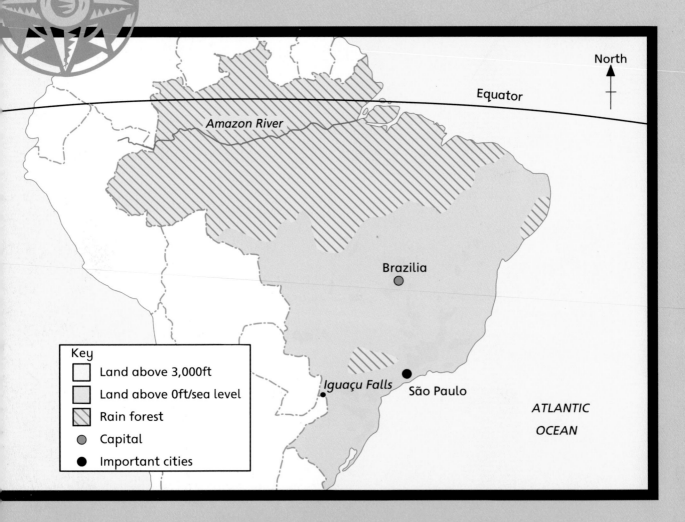

North

Equator

Amazon River

Brazilia

Iguaçu Falls São Paulo

ATLANTIC
OCEAN

Key
☐ Land above 3,000ft
☐ Land above 0ft/sea level
▨ Rain forest
● Capital
● Important cities

Brazil is in South America. It is the fifth
largest country in the world. The name
Brazil comes from the Brazil tree which
grows there and gives us Brazil nuts.

The first Brazilians were the **native Indians**. Then people came from all over the world. Brazilians eat, sleep, go to school, and play like you. Life in Brazil is also **unique**.

Land

Brazil has **rain forests**, rivers, **grasslands,** and beaches. Most of Brazil is south of the **equator**. Brazil has a **tropical climate**.

Brazil has more people and land than any other country in South America. Most Brazilians live in or around the cities.

The Amazon River flows through Brazil. It is the second largest river in the world. One thousand rivers run into the Amazon River.

Iguaçu Falls is in Brazil. It is one of the most beautiful **waterfalls** in the world. It is on the **border** between Brazil and Argentina.

Homes

Brasilia is the **capital** city, but São Paulo is Brazil's largest city. It is also one of the largest cities in the world.

Brazil has rich people but it has many more poor people. They live in **favelas** outside the big cities. There are some Brazilians who live in the **rain forest**.

Food

People have moved to Brazil from all around the world. They took with them many different **recipes**. Most of these use rice, beef, pork, fruit, vegetables, or beans.

Feijoada (fay-SHWA-dah) came from Africa and is very popular in Brazil. It is a stew of pork, beef, sausage, bacon, and black beans. It is served with sliced oranges.

13

Clothes

Brazil has a **tropical climate**. It is usually warm so people wear light, cool clothing. **Native Indians** wear **traditional** clothes in the wet **rain forest**.

Brazilians have many **festivals** and
holidays. This is when they dress up in
colorful clothes and costumes.

Work

Farmers in Brazil grow more sugarcane and coffee than any other country in the world. There are also many farmers or ranchers who have beef cattle.

Workers dig **iron ore** out of the ground to make steel. People in **factories** make steel, cloth, cars, and other **products**. Brazil sells many of these products to other countries.

Transportation

Brazilians travel by car, bus, and truck. In the crowded cities people share cars to save money and time.

The Amazon River is like a giant highway into the center of Brazil. There are very few roads in the Amazon **rain forest,** so people travel by boat and helicopter.

Language

Portuguese is Brazil's national language. Explorers from Portugal took it to Brazil 500 years ago. People also speak native Indian and African languages.

The first Brazilians were the **native Indians**. People from Europe began moving to Brazil 500 years ago. Africans were taken to Brazil as **slaves**. Today many people from Asia are moving to Brazil.

School

Most children go to school from ages six to sixteen. They study Portuguese, history, math, science, and art. Elementary school ends before noon each day.

Some Brazilian children are too poor to go to school. They must work to help feed their families.

Free Time

Soccer is called *futebol* (FOOT-bal). It is very popular in Brazil. All Brazilian children, rich and poor, play futebol.

Capoeira (cap-oh-AYR-a) is a Brazilian sport. It is like a fight, a dance, and judo all in one. Other popular sports are basketball, volleyball, tennis, and jogging.

Celebrations

Lemnaja (lem-NA-hah) is a Brazilian New Year's celebration. On New Year's Eve, people go to the beach to give presents to Lemnaja, the goddess of the sea.

Carnival is Brazil's biggest **festival**. It takes place about six weeks before Easter. There are **parades** through the noisy streets.

The Arts

Brazilians play music learned from the **native Indians**, Africans, and Europeans. People also like to play and sing *choros* (CHO-rose) or folk tunes.

The *berimbaus* (beh-RIM-bas) is a Brazilian **instrument**. It has one string and is played with a bow. Other popular instruments are guitars, banjos, drums, and maracas.

Fact File

Name	The full name of Brazil is the Federal Republic of Brazil.
Capital	The capital city is Brasilia.
Language	Most Brazilians speak Portuguese.
Population	There are 160 million people living in Brazil.
Money	Instead of the dollar, Brazilians have the *real* (ray-AHL).
Religions	Most Brazilians are Catholic or Protestant.
Products	Brazil produces more coffee and sugarcane than any other country.

Words You Can Learn

oi (oy)	hello
tchau (chow)	goodbye
obrigato (oh-bree-GAH-doh)	thank you
sim (seem)	yes
nao (na-oh)	no
um (oom)	one
dois (dah)	two
tres (trase)	three

Glossary

border	where two countries meet
capital	the city where the government is based
climate	the normal type of weather for the area
equator	an imaginary line around the earth dividing it into a northern half and a southern half
factories	places where things are made
favelas	large areas covered in small, roughly-made huts where people live
festival	a big celebration planned for many people to enjoy together
grasslands	large flat areas where grasses are the main plants that grow
instrument	something to make music with
iron ore	the rock which contains iron
native Indians	the first people who were living in Brazil
parade	a group of people performing or dancing while walking together
products	things which are grown, taken from the earth, made by hand, or made in a factory
rain forest	a thick forest that stays green all year and which has rain almost every day
recipe	a set of directions for making food
slave	a person who is taken from their home and family and sold to another person to do work
traditional	the way something has been done or made for a long time
tropical	hot and wet
unique	different in a special way
waterfall	where water falls down the side of a mountain

Index

More Books To Read

Cherry, Lynne. *The Great Kapok Tree*. Harcourt. 1990.

Cobb, Vicki. *This Place is Wet*. Walker. 1993.

Dawson, Zoe. *Postcards From Brazil*. Raintree Steck-Vaughn. 1996.

Haskins, Jim. *Count Your Way Through Brazil*. Carolrhoda. 1996.